Women Who Rape Men

John Davis, BA., J.D., LL.M.

Old Town Industries, Inc.
1978   Old Town Publishing

ISBN: - 13:978-1507702611

ISBN-10: 1507702612

DEDICATION

This monograph is dedicated to all who work with victims of rape and sexual assault.

William-Adolphe Bouguereau (1825–1905).
from "*Nymphs and Satyr*" (1873)

ACKNOWLEDGMENTS

The Author and Publisher would like to thank MGTOW Magazine.

Table of Contents

WOMEN WHO RAPE MEN

By: John Davis, BA., J.D., LL.M.

Although women are less inclined to use force in raping men, than men are inclined to use force in raping women, women frequently use drugs, deceit, positions of power and authority[1], and emotional manipulation to commit rape. Current studies indicate that women rape men and boys more often than the other way around.

These current studies contradict and correct the long held myths that men commit the "vast

---

[1] Christina Faulkner, MSW, RSW, Cheryl Regehr, PhD, "Sexual Boundary Violations Committed by Female Forensic Workers," 39 J.

majority" of rape, and, that women who rape are rare.

Recent studies have found that previous analyses of rape statistics, by those persons in government studies and NGO's, tend to be skewed because they focus only on male perpe-trators, or, because they overlook the intense discouragement society imposes on men who try to report women who rape.[2] Such studies are also skewed, to under-report female rapists of vulnerable males, because they focus on the in-tersection between professional authority and (mythical) male power in intimate relationships.[3]

In addition, other studies show that the inci-dence of male abuse of positions of authority or trust may be as low as 0.9 percent, and, that the incidence of female abuse of positions of au-thority or trust, to commit sexual crimes, may be as much as 3.1 percent (almost three and a half times as much as their male counterparts).[4]

---

[2] Sarah LaTrent, *"Against His Will-Female on Male Rape"* CNN Broadcast, October 10, 2013.
http://www.cnn.com/2013/10/09/living/chris-brown-female-on-male-rape/

[3] *Id.* at 154.

[4] *See,* Pope K: Sexual Involvement With Therapists. Washington, DC:

Still other studies show that men are more often

It is Rape

UNLESS HE CONSENTS

Se**X**ual Assault
Awareness Month

subjected to unwanted intercourse than women.

American Psychological Association, 1994.

In a 1998 study at California State University, researchers found that 70% of men had been subjected to sexual coercion by women within the preceding five years.[5] Overall, men are subjected to sexual coercion and unwanted intercourse 62.7% of the time, versus women being subjected to unwanted intercourse only 46.3% of the time in interpersonal relationships.[6] These statistics contradict established stereotypes in mainstream media's representations of men as being sexual aggressors, and, women assuming the role of refusing sex. Numerous other studies also dispel these erroneous mainstream stereotypes.

A recent (2002) study commissioned by the National Institute of Mental Health, and conducted by the University of Illinois details the dynamics of women who rape men.[7]

---

[5] Fiebert, M. S., & Tucci, Lisa M., Sexual coercion: Men Victimized by Women. 6 JOURNAL OF MEN'S STUDIES 2, pp. 127-133, 1998.

[6] Id.; Muehlenhard, C. L., & Cook, S. W. "Men's Self-Reports of Unwanted Sexual Activity." 24 JOURNAL OF SEX RESEARCH, 58-72, 1988. (This study seems particularly valid as the amount of statistical participants in the sample is relatively much higher than most comparable statistical studies. This study involved 507 men and 486 women [n = 993]).

[7] Debra L. Oswald, PhD, Brenda L. Russell, "Sexual Coercion and Victimization of College Men," 17 J. INTERPERSONAL VIOLENCE 3, pp. 273-285 (March 2002). (One hundred and seventy-three men were recruited from undergraduate courses at a private Midwestern Uni-

Only recently have researchers begun to examine sexual coercion directed toward men [citations omitted] Struckman-Johnson (1988)[8] and Struckman-Johnson (1998)[9] found 43% of men sampled reported experiencing a coercive incident, of which 36% reported unwanted touch and 27% reported being coerced into sexual intercourse. Research examining both men and women as perpetrators and victims of coercive or aggressive behavior found that men and women experience comparable levels of physical violence in dating relationships (McConaghy & Zamir, 1995;[10] Sigelman, Berry, & Wiles, 1984)[11]. . . . . These studies reveal that victimization of men occurs with some regularity; . . . .[12]

---

versity. Mean age of respondents was 20.94 (SD = 3.48). (n=173).

[8] Struckman-Johnson, C., "Forced sex on dates: It happens to men too." 24 JOURNAL OF SEX RESEARCH 234-241 (1988).

[9] Struckman-Johnson, C., & Struckman-Johnson, D. "The dynamics and impact of sexual coercion of men by women." In P. B. Anderson, & C. Struckman-Johnson (Eds.), "Sexually aggressive women: Current perspectives and controversies" (pp. 121-143). New York: Guilford.

[10] McConaghy, N., & Zamir, R., "Heterosexual and homosexual coercion, sexual orientation and sexual roles in medical students." 24 ARCHIVES OF SEXUAL BEHAVIOR, 489-502 (1995).

[11] Sigelman, C. K., Berry, C. J., & Wiles, K. A. "Violence in college students' dating relationships," 5 JOURNAL OF APPLIED SOCIAL PSYCHOLOGY, 530-548 (1984).

[12] Oswald & Russell, *supra* at 274.

These studies show that 27% of college men have been raped by women by the time they were of college age. (I.e., according to the new federal definitions of rape, the men have been subjected to coerced intercourse without their consent).[13]

Given the predominant stereotypes in mainstream media, literature and entertainment, it is apparent that men are being wrongfully demonized as stereotypical rapists in our culture. Men, are, in fact, victims of rape by women on a regular basis, and, to a greater extent than women being victims of men.

Rape and Female Sex Predators

According to the Center for Disease Control [CDC] Women who rape men, children and other women, are becoming increasingly more common.

(It is perhaps more than symbolic to note

---

[13] United States Department of Justice, *An Updated Definition of Rape*, http://blogs.justice.gov/main/archives/1801 January 6, 2012.

that Dr. Kimberly Quinlan Lindsey, 44, a Deputy Director of the CDC, was arrested after a six-week investigation into allegations she molested a six-year old boy. Lindsey has been arrested and charged with two counts of child molestation and one count of bestiality, according to a DeKalb County (Georgia) criminal complaint).[14]

This dramatic increase in the numbers of women who are rapists and sex offenders has drawn the concern of NGO's and women leaders across the U.S.

Only a Few Women Commit Sex Crimes

---

[14] http://www.cnn.com/2011/10/11/justice/georiga-cdc-arrest/

Notwithstanding the dramatic increase in the number of women who rape, many Americans still have the misconception that a woman cannot rape a man, a boy, another woman or a girl.

A definition from the Oxford English Dictionary provides the common meaning (and understanding) of the word "rape" in modern culture. That definition reads:

rape

Syllabification: rape

Pronunciation: /rāp /

NOUN

1The crime, typically committed by a man, of forcing another person to have sexual intercourse with the offender against their will: *he denied two charges of attempted rape he had committed at least two rapes*

SYNONYMS

1.1*ARCHAIC* The abduction of a woman, especially for the purpose of having sexual intercourse with her: *the Rape of the Sabine Women*

2The wanton destruction or spoiling of a place or area: *the rape of the Russian countryside*

This common usage definition of "rape" is not adequate to address all of the problems of rape. This definition and common understanding of rape is gender specific and misleads people into believing that only men can be rapists, and, that only women can be victims of rape. This common meaning of the word "rape" is misandrist (hateful of men) in that it does not extend the awareness of the horrors of rape to men or boys who are victims of rape by women.

This common definition of rape persists in media, in common usage, and in the misperceptions of the public. These false stereotypes, unfortunately, minimize the seriousness of the injuries caused women who rape and molest boys and men.

In an effort to address the problem of rape, especially with men and boys as victims, the United States has finally, after almost 100 years, updated its definition of rape to include men and boys as victims.

The new federal definition of rape is:

> *"The penetration, no matter how slight, of the vagina or anus with any body part or object, or oral penetration by a sex organ of another person, without the consent of the victim."*

"For the first time, ever, the new definition includes any gender of victim and perpetrator, not just women being raped by men."

These new definitions, at the federal level,

are likely to lead to the compilation of more accurate federal statistics on the number of female predators who commit rape.

Experts estimate, however, that it will take at least several years before the new federal definitions will start to have an impact on increasing the accuracy of government and NGO rape statistics in the U.S.

The new federal definition of rape has been implemented to adopt to the gender-neutral definitions of rape that already exists in most state statutes.

A complete legal analysis of rape statutes, in the various states, is beyond the scope of this book. It may be helpful, however, for readers to have an example of one of the state statutes criminalizing rape.

California's penal code, for example, contains the following definition of "rape." A simplified explanation of the legalese will follow.

> *CAL. PEN. CODE § 261 : California Code - Section 261*
>
> *(a)Rape is an act of sexual intercourse accomplished with a person not the spouse of the perpetrator, under any of the following circumstances:*
>
> *(1)Where a person is incapable, because of a*

mental disorder or developmental or physical disability, of giving legal consent, and this is known or reasonably should be known to the person committing the act. Notwithstanding the existence of a conservatorship pursuant to the provisions of the Lanterman-Petris-Short Act (Part 1 (commencing with Section 5000) of Division 5 of the Welfare and Institutions Code), the prosecuting attorney shall prove, as an element of the crime, that a mental disorder or developmental or physical disability rendered the alleged victim incapable of giving consent.

(2)Where it is accomplished against a person's will by means of force, violence, duress, menace, or fear of immediate and unlawful bodily injury on the person or another.

(3)Where a person is prevented from resisting by any intoxicating or anesthetic substance, or any controlled substance, and this condition was known, or reasonably should have been known by the accused.

(4)Where a person is at the time unconscious of the nature of the act, and this is known to the accused. As used in this paragraph, "unconscious of the nature of the act" means incapable of resisting because the victim meets one of the following conditions:

(A)Was unconscious or asleep.
(B)Was not aware, knowing, perceiving, or cognizant that the act occurred.
(C)Was not aware, knowing, perceiving, or cognizant of the essential characteristics of the act due to the perpetrator's fraud in fact.
(D)Was not aware, knowing, perceiving, or cognizant of the essential characteristics of the act due to the perpetrator's fraudulent repre-

sentation that the sexual penetration served a professional purpose when it served no professional purpose.

(5)Where a person submits under the belief that the person committing the act is the victim's spouse, and this belief is induced by any artifice, pretense, or concealment practiced by the accused, with intent to induce the belief.

(6)Where the act is accomplished against the victim's will by threatening to retaliate in the future against the victim or any other person, and there is a reasonable possibility that the perpetrator will execute the threat. As used in this paragraph, "threatening to retaliate" means a threat to kidnap or falsely imprison, or to inflict extreme pain, serious bodily injury, or death.

(7)Where the act is accomplished against the victim's will by threatening to use the authority of a public official to incarcerate, arrest, or deport the victim or another, and the victim has a reasonable belief that the perpetrator is a public official. As used in this paragraph, "public official" means a person employed by a governmental agency who has the authority, as part of that position, to incarcerate, arrest, or deport another. The perpetrator does not actually have to be a public official.

(b)As used in this section, "duress" means a direct or implied threat of force, violence, danger, or retribution sufficient to coerce a reasonable person of ordinary susceptibilities to perform an act which otherwise would not have been performed, or acquiesce in an act to which one otherwise would not have submitted. The total circumstances, including the age of the victim, and his or her relationship to the defendant, are fac-

tors to consider in appraising the existence of duress.

(c)As used in this section, "menace" means any threat, declaration, or act which shows an intention to inflict an injury upon another.

The first paragraph in this law, paragraph "(a)," contains the essence of a charge of rape. Rape is the act of sexual intercourse, with another person whose is not a spouse, without the consent of the other person. The law then goes on to define seven specific definitions of what is not consent.

The law is "gender neutral." It recognizes that either a man, or a woman, may be convicted of rape if one of the participants in sexual intercourse does not consent to the intercourse.

The seven numbered sub-paragraphs define specific cases in which a victim of rape has not given consent (as a matter of law).

(1)   Mental or physical impairment;

(2)   Use of force or threat of bodily injury;

(3)   Impairment from any substance that affects a person's will;

(4)   One of the participants in the sexual intercourse is unconscious of the fact

that they are being subjected to physical sex;

(5)   One of the participants believes (for any reason) that the other participant is their spouse;

(6)   One of the participants engages in sexual intercourse because of a threat of retaliation;

(7)   One of the participants is a public official (such as a policewoman) and threatens to use their authority to arrest, imprison or deport someone unless they have intercourse.

As with many state statutes, this rape statute is not as broad and all encompassing as the new federal definition. It is, however, representative of current state laws which criminalize what our legal system previously termed: "first degree rape."

Many other countries include oral copulation among their criminalization of sexual activities as "first degree rape."

In the following sections are applications of the concepts of rape and sexual assault applied to case studies of actual (or alleged) female sex predators.

How Do Women Rape Men?

There are many myths surrounding the phenomenon of women raping men.

Many people still have the mistaken impression that it is physically impossible for a woman to rape a man because a woman does not have a penis.

What this misconception overlooks is that a woman can force her vagina over a man's penis (known as *"forced envelopment"* or *"forced to penetrate"*), or, a woman can use threats, emotional manipulation, drugs, alcohol, and a variety of other means to induce a man to penetrate her vagina. This latter phenomenon is known as *"made to penetrate rape."*

Both *forced envelopment*, and, *made to penetrate*, are first-degree rape under the modern laws of most jurisdictions.

Women can also rape a man by using an object, or one of her body parts, to penetrate his anus. This is a very common method women use to rape young boys. Keeping in mind that rape is not just about sex, but is about power, many female sex predators feel that humiliating a man or boy, by anal penetration, is a form of domination and exercising power and control over the victim. It is rape.

Oral copulation is another form women use to rape men. Most civilized western nations have now recognized that a woman who uses her mouth, or hand, to stimulate a man's penis or anus, without his consent, have committed rape.

Many also still have the misconception that because women are physically weaker than men, that they cannot rape a man against his will.

The fact is that men are conditioned, from early in their infancy, to never physically use force on women. Consequently, it is relatively easy for a woman to use force to rape a man. Most physicians and experts on rape advise that many, many men, while being raped by a woman, simply freeze. Estimates are that 60% of men who are raped by women, freeze during the rape.

Women who rape also frequently use drugs and alcohol to diminish the capacity of a man or boy to resist, or defend himself, against a woman rapist. Many of the news articles on female teachers who rape young boys include descriptions of how the rapist plied the young boys with drugs or alcohol in order to overcome their natural resistance, and natural sense of boundaries.

Some are also under the mistaken belief that a man cannot be raped because a man cannot have an erection unless he consents to a woman enveloping his penis with her mouth or vagina. However, medical science tells us that an erection, and even penile ejaculation, is a physical reflex. It is not something that is always under the direct control of a man's consciousness. In fact, a man can be completely unconscious, even comatose, and still have a complete erection, and, still be able to climax or ejaculate. This should be obvious from the fact that most (if not all) male children, experience nocturnal emissions during their adolescence.

What is clear is not that women cannot rape men, but, that women have been raping men since the beginning of time and we are only now beginning to recognize women as rapists.

Rape and Paternity Fraud

On the leading edge of the concept of women who rape men involves womyn's use of fraud to obtain a man's consent to vaginal sex.

Paternity fraud comes in many forms. The most common form is for a woman to obtain a man's consent to marriage by fraudulently telling him that she is pregnant when she is not.

However, there are a variety of other forms of paternity fraud. One, for example, involves a woman telling a man she has does not want to become pregnant, but, at the same time, she is fully planning on becoming pregnant from the intercourse. This is not a difficult fraud to accomplish.

For example, in one case, a man used a condom during intercourse with a woman. However, the woman used the sperm in the discarded condom, after the man had left, to impregnate herself. The man would not have had intercourse with the woman if he had known that she was planning on the creepy conduct of impregnating herself with the discarded sperm.[15]

Is this rape?

Let's examine the California rape statute we quoted above. The statute contains an express provision in which sex becomes rape if the victim is under the influence of a woman's fraud:

> (4)Where a person is at the time unconscious of the nature of the act, and this is known to the accused. As used in this paragraph, "unconscious of the nature of the act" means incapable of resisting because the victim meets one of the

---

[15] "Woman Steals Ex-Boyfriend's Sperm, Has Twins, Sues for Child Support ... and WINS!" The Liberty Crier, September 28, 2014. http://libertycrier.com/woman-steals-ex-boyfriends-sperm-twins-sues-child-support-wins/

following conditions: . . .

. . . .

> *(C)Was not aware, knowing, perceiving, or cognizant of the essential characteristics of the act due to the perpetrator's fraud in fact.*

Telling a man that you want to have intercourse with him but don't want to get pregnant (by engaging in sex with a condom) while planning to steal the man's sperm for insemination is arguably "fraud in fact." As most attorneys are aware, fraud voids consent. Consequently, in a case like the one described above, the woman arguably committed first degree rape by obtaining the man's participation in sex under false pretenses (fraud).

One of the most common examples of paternity fraud involve a woman engaging a man in an intimate relationship while she is having sex with another man, or men. It is common for womyn to lie to a man about the actual father of a child with which she is pregnant. Womyn often lie to men in sexual relationships about the man being the "only one" in order to secure his consent to marriage and continuing sex.

Arguably, this is pure fraud on the man, and voids his consent to the sex in which he engages with the rapist. She becomes a rapist because of her fraud on the man regarding her faithfulness to the relationship in order to secure his continuing intimacy (and economic support).

Most paternity can now be rather easily established with economical DNA testing at birth. It is wise beyond comprehension for men NOT to sign as the father on a birth certificate, until he has obtained a paternity test of the child, to insure that he is, in fact, the father of the child.

Some jurisdictions are considering legislation making paternity tests mandatory at birth. However, so far, most gynocentric jurisdictions have rejected this legislation. The French national assembly is among the most prominent of the countries to reject mandatory paternity testing laws. In fact, France is so misandrist and gynocentric as to ban paternity testing.[16]

Lying With Rape Statistics – Rape Statistic Propaganda

---

[16] *"Paternity Testing Ban Upheld in France,"* International Biosciences, http://www.ibdna.com/regions/UK/EN/?page=paternity-testing-ban-upheld-in-france%22paternity.

Another more global rape fraud involves the false claim that male victims of rape are rare, that women are at high risk for rape, and that all men are rapists.

Of all the statistics available in the information age, rape statistics are the most elusive.

Statistics on rape are inherently unreliable because of the political and gynocentric interests that stand to gain from exaggerating the amount of rape that occurs.

Rape is considered such a serious crime, that a mere accusation of rape is sufficient to ruin an accused. Consequently, the power to falsely accuse of rape is a coveted power. It enables someone to invoke massive law enforcement resources based upon a mere accusation, and, it empower someone to inflict immense injury on a falsely accused without having to comply with due process. (Even though a majority of rape accusations are proven to be false, the mere accusation and arrest of an innocent person on rape charges is sufficient to make that person unemployable, and, a semi-permanent subject of hatred and scorn in any community).

The result is that gynocentric interests (ridiculously) exaggerate the number of actual rapes that occur.

This exaggeration of the incidence of rape in the U.S. reached hysterical proportions in 2013 and 2014, and, eventually the mainstream media began to question the hysteria.

Our research for this work indicates that there are some reliable statistics available on the real incidence of rape. However, there are almost no reliable analyses of those rape statistics available.

The FBI has published an often suppressed statistic on the incidence of rape in the U.S. The FBI's statistic is that the incidence of rape is 26.9 rapes per 100,000 people in the U.S. Based upon a population estimate of 313,914,040 people in the United States, there were, in 2012, approximately 84,443 forcible rapes **reported** in the U.S.

Although this is a "hard statistic," and would seem to indicate that there were 84,443 forcible rapes in the U.S. in 2012, it is important to realize that not all "reported rapes" constitute actual rape.

In determining the actual rate of rape, in the U.S., one must take some factors into consideration.

The first factor is the amount of false rape

reports. Our research conclusively established that roughly 60% of "reported rapes" are false.

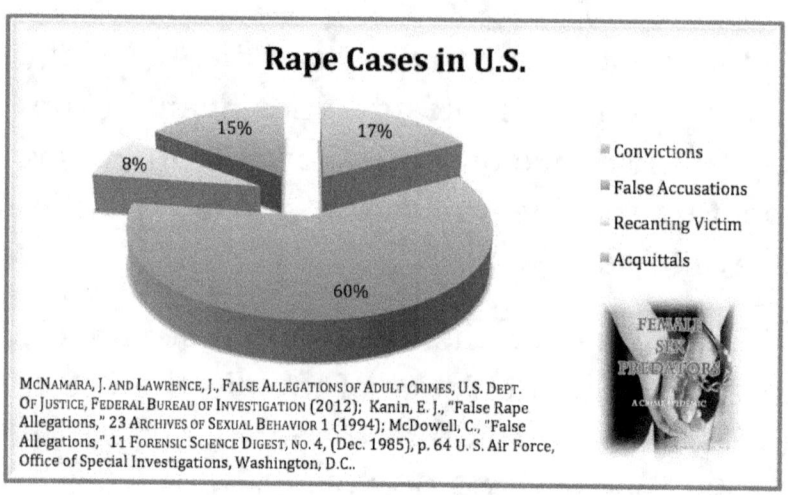

Rape Cases in U.S.

17%
15%
8%
60%

Convictions
False Accusations
Recanting Victim
Acquittals

MCNAMARA, J. AND LAWRENCE, J., FALSE ALLEGATIONS OF ADULT CRIMES, U.S. DEPT. OF JUSTICE, FEDERAL BUREAU OF INVESTIGATION (2012); Kanin, E. J., "False Rape Allegations," 23 ARCHIVES OF SEXUAL BEHAVIOR 1 (1994); McDowell, C., "False Allegations," 11 FORENSIC SCIENCE DIGEST, NO. 4, (Dec. 1985), p. 64 U. S. Air Force, Office of Special Investigations, Washington, D.C..

About half of the rapes that are taken to trial result in acquittals, and another 8% of "reported rapes" result in the accuser recanting the accusation of rape, or, DNA evidence exonerates the accused.

The chart above shows the statistical adjustments that must be made to the number of "reported rapes" in order to arrive at an accurate number of actual forcible rapes.

Realistically, only 17% of "reported rape" cases are actual cases of rape. This would seem to indicate that the actual number of rapes occurring in the U.S. in 2012 was 14,355 rapes. That figure yields an adjusted statistical probability of a woman being raped, in a given year, at one in 11,371.

However, to arrive at an accurate figure of rape, one must make another major adjustment.

The FBI statistics do NOT include the numbers of women who rape men in which men are the victims and women are the offenders. The numbers of women who rape men have been intentionally excluded from federal statistics up until January of 2012.

Contemporary Media Recognition – Women Who Rape Men

It has only been in the past few years, that mainstream media has given any attention to women who rape men.

However, many major media news feeds are beginning to recognize the problem.

Prior to about 2014, mainstream media often assisted in disseminating myths about women who rape. Prior to any broadcast program, news or magazine article, editors would often insist on stock language to the extent that women who rape are in very small numbers.

Recent mainstream articles, however, have finally begun illuminating the full extent of the problem of women who are rapists.

In a column on September 23, 2014, a courageous author finally published an historic article in a mainstream media news outlet that underscores the pervasive reality of women who rape.[17]

Glenn Harlan Reynolds, finally conquered the mass denial in the mainstream media and published a well-documented column on the prevalence of women who rape as being greater than men who rape women.

Comment in the article, Mr. Reynolds noted:

> *According to a recent study from the University of Missouri* [18] *published by the American Psy-*

[17] Glenn Harlan Reynolds, "*A rape epidemic — by women?*" U.S.A. Today, September 23, 2014.
http://www.usatoday.com/story/opinion/2014/09/22/rape-cdc-numbers-misleading-definition-date-forced-sexual-assault-column/16007089/

[18] Bryana H. French, Jasmine D. Tilghman, Dominique A. Malebranche. **Sexual Coercion Context and Psychosocial Correlates Among Diverse Males.**. *Psychology of Men & Masculinity*, 2014;

chological Association, male victims are often victimized by women: "A total of 43% of high school boys and young college men reported they had an unwanted sexual experience and of those, 95% said a female acquaintance was the aggressor, according to a study published online in the APA journal Psychology of Men and Masculinity."[19]

Though delayed by centuries of ignorance on the subject of rape, law enforcement, the media, and the public are finally becoming aware that female sex predators represent a serious and substantial concern to our culture.

Healing After Awareness:

Most men are not aware that they have been raped, until the trauma of the rape forces them out of denial into the light of awareness. This process often takes 20 years or more.

One of the most painful experiences for men,

DOI: 10.1037/a0035915

19

http://old.sciencedaily.com/releases/2014/03/140325113302.htm

if they decide to confide in someone that they have been raped by a woman, is that they will be met with disbelief, derision, confusion and frequently hostility.

Although Billions of dollars have been spent on training law enforcement to be responsive to women who claim to be victims of rape, there has literally been no funding for training law enforcement to respond, sensitively, to male victims of rape. Law enforcement is likely to turn their backs on boys or men who have been raped by women.

For these reasons, men simply do not report, to anyone, that a woman has raped them.

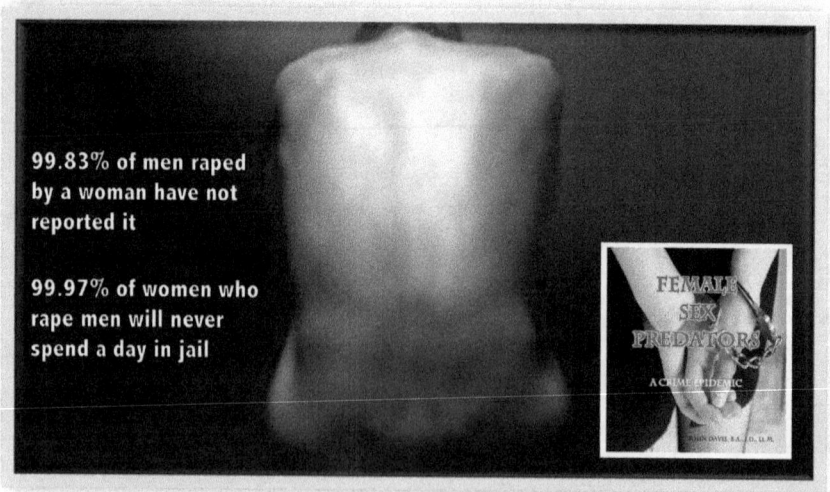

99.83% of men raped by a woman have not reported it

99.97% of women who rape men will never spend a day in jail

FEMALE SEX PREDATORS

A CRIME EPIDEMIC

Most men who are victims of rape and abuse by womyn will repress the memory of the trauma.

It is usually only in later years that men begin to develop symptoms of abuse that are so severe they command attention and denial becomes impossible.

Men who have been sexually abused by womyn are almost twice as likely to have physical (medical problems) such as heart disease, cardio-pulmonary disease, post-traumatic stress disorder (PTSD), and a variety of other symptoms that become inescapable as male victims approach middle age.

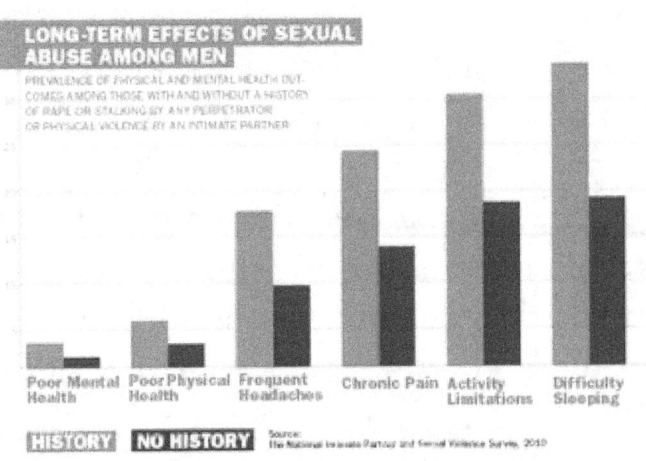

Men who have been raped by women often become socially isolated, depressed, subject to anxiety (panic) attacks, and, like most victims of rape, are subject to intense confusion and chaotic emotions.

It is challenging for professionals to attempt to describe what happens when a man is raped by a woman. The most severe injury to the man is a loss of a sense of boundaries. This is particularly true of boys who are raped by women. This loss of boundaries not only applies to the man or boy's sense of external boundaries, but also the man or boy's senses of internal boundaries.

The man or boy rape victim will find it difficult to adjust his boundaries with others. He may, unknowingly set himself up for further sexual assaults by women. He may find it difficult or impossible to be sexually assertive in relationships – he may find it difficult to say "no." This loss of personal boundaries may find its way into his normal friendships, his business and professional relationships, and, most certainly, into any of his intimate relationships. Men who are victims of women who rape are likely to be terrified of intimacy.

Part of this terror of intimacy derives from the post-traumatic nature of rape injuries. Each time a man or boy, who has been raped by a woman, engages in PIV ("penis in vagina") intercourse, he is likely to relive the trauma of the time he is raped. This can happen even if he is having intercourse with a woman he thoroughly loves and trusts. It is important for women attempting to help a male survivor of rape to understand that his fear and terror is not necessarily about her, but about the trauma he relives each time he engages in normal sex.

In terms of a loss of internal boundaries, the man or boy who has been raped by a woman has a difficult time sorting through emotions. He may have simultaneous and contradictory emotions within himself in intimate relationships. For example, a rape survivor will often use anger and other outbursts to suppress feelings of helplessness, grief, humiliation or emotional pain from memories of having been raped.

Instead of feeling these emotions sequentially, the man or boy who is a victim of rape may feel these emotions at the same time. Often the male rape victim will feel that he is "falling apart" and be completely helpless in identifying the source of the chaotic emotional quandary which is tormenting him.

Although sensitive and caring family members, friends, spouses and paramours can often help a man through these difficult episodes, **it is critical that a male survivor seek and find professional help**.

Unfortunately, although tens of billions of dollars are spent on assisting women rape victims, there are few programs for male survivors. Unfortunately, professional assistance for men who are rape survivors, is not often capable of addressing the unique issues that men face when recovering from women who rape.

Seeking and Finding Professional Assistance

In a perfect world, all professionals are equal, and all professionals are able to help all patients with all problems.

In the real world, the effectiveness of a professional, whether it is a lawyer, doctor, psychologist or spiritual advisor, depends on many, many variables. In addition, in the real world, professional intervention is frequently costly.

As our culture advances in its awareness of men and boys who are victims of women who rape, it may become increasingly possible for men to report rape to authorities, and, have those reports be taken with sensitivity and seriousness. As difficult as it may be for a male rape survivor, it is important that the survivor consider reporting the rape to authorities.

The principle reason for reporting rape by women is that a victim of a crime is often accorded certain rights, as a victim, that may help to ameliorate the devastating effects of the crime of rape. For example, if a woman is convicted of raping a man, as part of her criminal sentence, the Court should order the rapist to pay for medical and psychological services to assist the man or boy in recovering.

Absent an order in a criminal sentence, the boy or man, who survives a woman's rape, may be able to file suit against the woman (and any accomplices) to recover the funds necessary for the survivor to successfully complete medical and psychological treatment (which can often take years to complete).

During the process of looking for professional help, the male rape survivor should engage a temporary strategy to facilitate his success in finding help. A helpful strategy and temporary plan for most male rape survivors includes:

1. Nurture yourself – take care of yourself; give yourself the time and permission to heal; give yourself the health resources you need to walk the path that you are on.

2. Go easy on yourself- the greatest hazard a man faces in seeking help as a rape victim is to overcome the delusion that it was your fault; **it is never your fault**.

3. Patience – give yourself the time you need to recover and find the help you need; this process can take years. Take baby steps.

4. Flexibility – A survivor is on a difficult path as a rape survivor – a survivor must expect to stumble. A survivor can make it through if he backs up when he hits obstacles and tries a different approach when he needs to do so.

5. Curiosity – You might feel the need to know everything about your recovery. Resist the temptation to think that you know everything about it. As a survivor of a woman rapist you will need to learn many new things about yourself, about the world around you, and about the people in your world. Be careful who you let into you circle of confidants. Take your time learning to

trust those to whom you are looking for help.

6. Humility – What happened to you is beyond your control. You cannot change the past. At the same time, you cannot blame yourself for what someone else did to you at your expense. The best you can do is accept what happened, and use it as an opportunity to find new people, and new paths in your life, to heal and grow stronger.

There is Hope

For men recovering from being raped by a woman, the road can seem impassible at times.

What was once life may seem, to victims of rape, to become an impossible burden. Some men do not survive. In the United States, men commit suicide at a rate four times higher than women. Much of those disturbing statistics are, in part, due to women who rape men.

Once a rape victim realizes that they are the victim of a dastardly crime committed upon them, rage is one of the most difficult burdens to endure in that interval between awareness and healing. A rape survivor must guard against that rage turning inwards on themselves.

A rape survivor must also sustain hope in the process of finding professional assistance. Many men have come through the healing and recovery process. There is always hope that someone will help.

As difficult as the world may seem, as much misandry (hatred of men) exists in our culture, there are still many people who are willing to be sensitive to men who are surviving a rape experience by a woman. Like any other any hero in an epic tale, the rape survivor needs to keep going along the road to recovery and know that there are those who will help him along the way.

COMING SOON

ALSO AVAILABLE

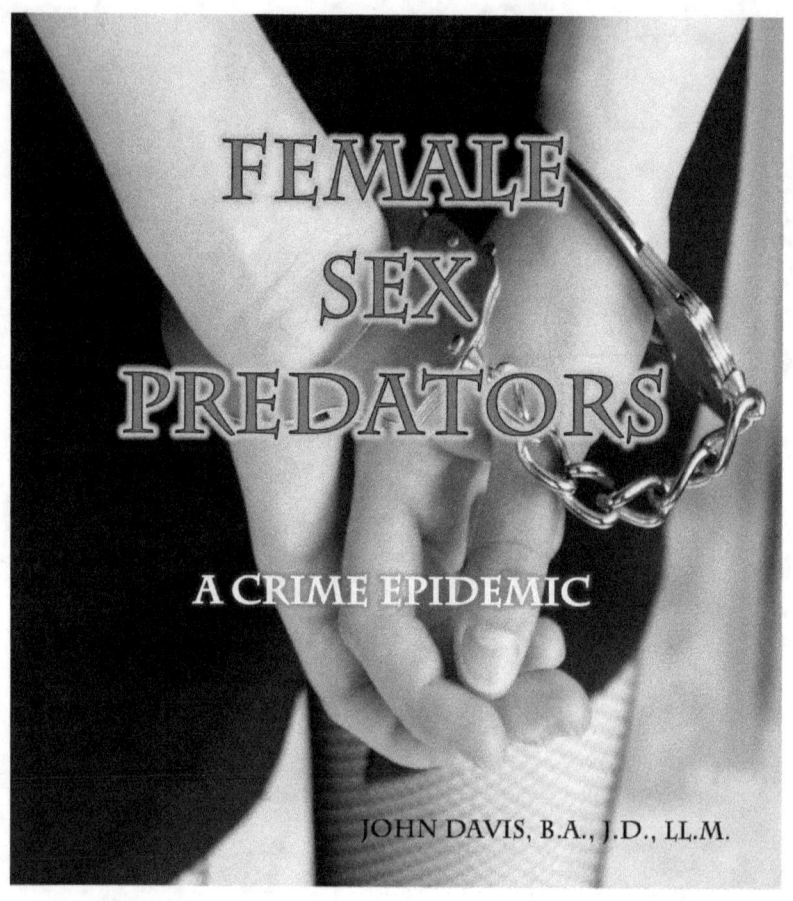

ABOUT THE AUTHOR

John Davis (1953 -) was born in Cleveland, Ohio. He was educated at Case Western Reserve University (BA) (one of the top ten universities in the United States), Seattle University School of Law (JD), and, New York University School of Law (LL.M post-doctoral) (one of the top ten law schools in the United States). John is fluent in seven languages (including ancient Latin and Greek). He has travelled the world over, many times, and has represented clients, in his thirty five year career, such as the United States Government and the Federation of Russia.

He has been a prosecutor three times in his 35 year career. He has held positions such as Assistant Attorney General (State of Arizona), United States Speaker, and Deputy District Attorney.

For most of his career in civil law, John was a successful international lawyer, practicing in many nations around the world.

John is now retired and lives in the South of France.